BITCOIN AND CRYPTOCURRENCY

Blockchain Technologies, Volume 1

rodney cannon

Published by rodney cannon, 2018.

While every precaution has been taken in the preparation of this book, the publisher assumes no responsibility for errors or omissions, or for damages resulting from the use of the information contained herein.

BITCOIN AND CRYPTOCURRENCY

First edition. March 19, 2018.

Copyright © 2018 rodney cannon.

Written by rodney cannon.

BITCOIN AND CRYPTOCURRENCY
WHAT YOU NEED TO KNOW ABOUT BITCOIN CRYPTOCURRENCiES AND BLOCKCHAIN TECHNOLOGY
By.
Rodney Cannon

CHAPTER ONE BITCOIN 101

BITCOIN AND CRYPTOCURRENCY

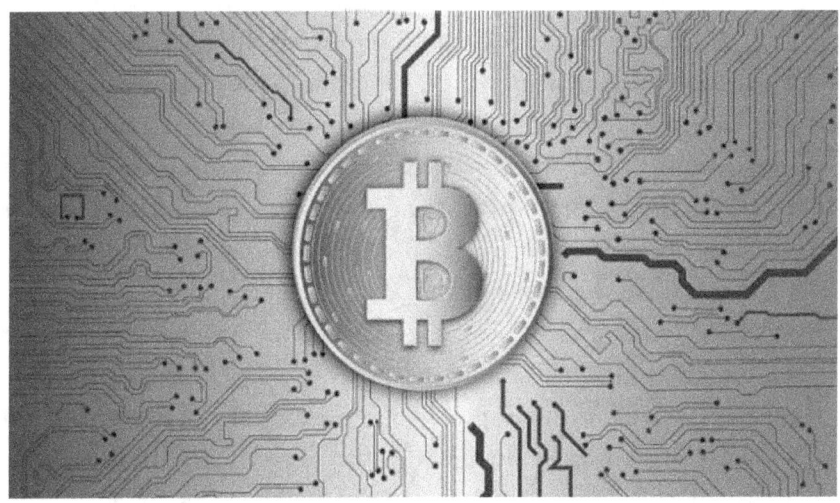

- I'm interested in things that change the world or that affect the future and wondrous, new technology where you see it, and you're like, 'Wow, how did that even happen? How is that possible?'- Elon Musk

While new technologies have the ability to elicit online debates and stir controversy while baffling a majority of the population, none has been able to do that with such vigor as the cryptocurrencies, and Bitcoin to be specific. This virtual currency has been a constant source of interest and confusion since it thrust itself into the mainstream more than 5 years ago. Amazingly, the cryptocurrency has experienced massive growth in the last few years, and its value is now greater than ever.

I know, all the above might be quite challenging to grasp, and this is why we've compiled this guide that will help you understand Bitcoin better. This guide will shine a light to looking to know what is Bitcoin, how you can get it, and expound on the properties of this cryptocurrency, without necessarily floundering into the technical details of this virtual coin.

Read on.

What Is Bitcoin?

Before we even get to understand the meaning of the term Bitcoin, it would be prudent that we first have a rudimentary understanding of the term cryptocurrency, since Bitcoin, is a subset of cryptocurrency.

Cryptocurrency

A cryptocurrency is a line of computer generated code that holds monetary value. These computer coded lines are developed using electricity and high-performance computers.

Also known as digital/virtual currency, cryptocurrencies are a form of public digital money that is generated using complex mathematical algorithms, and oversighted by millions of computer users known as "miners."

Being digital currencies, they created and held electronically, on a computer, and they're not available in a physical form like dollars, euros, or Yen.

Bitcoin

Bitcoin is a cryptocurrency, meaning it's digital/virtual money. Bitcoin was developed by a mysterious developer, who uses a pseudonym

Satoshi Nakamoto, and the coins exploded on to the financial scene in 2013, following enormous increase in their value.

In the original Bitcoin whitepaper, Nakamoshi describes his project as a "peer to peer version of electronic cash", which can be translated as a form of money transfer that does not involve going through the financial institutions.

Unlike other forms of monetary items, Bitcoin does not flow through the traditional banking system, rather, it flows from one electronic wallet, also known as an e-wallet, to another.

Amazing Properties of Bitcoin

But why Bitcoin and not other forms of cryptocurrencies?

If you're still wondering why this currency has made such an impact in the last half a decade, it's because it has some positive or rather cool attributes that make it so popular.

And yes, I agree, there are other forms of virtual currencies that can facilitate online transactions, including the Fiat digital currencies. But what really separates Bitcoin from other digital currencies?

Let's look at some of the amazing properties of Bitcoin.

1) Pseudonymous

Unlike the traditional forms of money transfer where senders or receivers are usually identified either for verification purposes or complying with anti-laundering or other legislation, users of Bitcoin operate in semi-anonymity.

The anonymity attribute occurs since there's no central "validator", meaning that users do not have the need to identify themselves for a successful transaction.

In practice, users are usually identified using their e-wallet address. While this might make it possible to analyze the transaction flow, it's not necessarily possible to connect the real-world identity of the users, and this has made Bitcoin an easy target for money-launders, and criminals.

2) Decentralization

The decentralization of the Bitcoin is among its most unique characteristic. With a decentralized system, no institution, or state can control the currency. Not even the central bank can control the currency, meaning that it has complete autonomy, compared to other currencies, and it's not affected by political, social or economic conditions of a country.

This has caused quite a controversy, and uneasiness among many states, such as China, owing to the fact that the governments feel uncomfortable with a currency that they've no power over.

3) Limited Supply

Yes, unlike Fiat currencies, which have an unlimited supply and central banks can issue as many as they want and even try to manipulate a currency's' value relative to others, Bitcoins are available in limited supply.

See, mining of Bitcoins is tightly controlled using an algorithm, and at the current rate, experts agree that the mining will continue at a diminishing rate until There is a maximum value of 21 is attained, and will no longer have Bitcoins.

4) Immutability

Unlike electronic Fiat transactions, Bitcoin transactions are irreversible. This is to mean that once you click the send button, the Bitcoin is gone, and gone forever, and nobody can reverse that transaction, not even the miner.

While this can cause disquiet among some users, it also means that any transaction on the Bitcoin network cannot be tampered with.

5) Divisibility

The smallest unit of a Bitcoin is known as a Satoshi and is a hundred millionth of a Bitcoin (0.0000001), approximately a hundredth of a cent. Such divisibility of the Bitcoin, allows users to perform microtransactions, that Fiat currencies cannot.

Where to Find Bitcoins

Now that you are aware of the merits and demerits of Bitcoin solely based on its attributes, it's time to look at where you can get genuine Bitcoin.

-The first way is to mine Bitcoins. Anybody can do that, provided you have electricity and high-performance computers. You should be aware that this method is capital intensive though.

-The second method is to buy the coins from trusted sellers such as LocalBitcoin.

-You can also cryptocurrency exchange markets such as Coinbase and Coinsquare, where you can exchange your "regular" coins with Bitcoins.

-Finally, you can sell your products/services to sellers who accept Bitcoins as a means of payment.

Is Bitcoin A Bubble Yet To Burst?

In the recent past, cryptocurrency prices have plummeted, with Bitcoin getting the hardest hit of all. But does this mean that Bitcoin was just a hoax?

Well, I don't think so; firstly, a bubble does not take so long before it bursts. Bitcoin is 2/3 years shy of hitting a decade since inception, and I don't think hoax can stay for that long. Secondly, we've seen big names- the who is who in the financial domain investing in this currency, and I think they wouldn't do so if it was just a bubble. Finally, some of the federal governments and prominent enterprises have acknowledged the money and are now using it as a form of payment.

CHAPTER TWO THE FIRST CONTROVERSIAL CURRENCY

BITCOIN AND CRYPTOCURRENCY 9

-When Henry Ford made cheap, reliable cars people said, 'Nah, what's wrong with a horse?' That was a huge bet he made, and it worked.- Elon Musk

The idea of paper currency was first developed during the 7th century under the Shang Dynasty in China.China's implementation of paper currency turned out to be very influential across the globe.Marco Polo, an explorer for Europe, brought the concept of paper currency to the people of his continent in the 13th century. In the early part of the 1800's, Napoleon issued paper currency. Also, the original paper currency were receipts for a value on an account.

How paper currency is perceived has changed as the centuries progressed. Prior to the inception of paper currency, money was represented by valuable metals. On the other hand, paper currency was viewed as a receipt or a promise to compensate a person with metal. Eventually, valuable metals were eliminated from the monetary system, which led to paper currency becoming fiat money. Fiat money is currency that is assigned value by a government and doesn't have any traits that make it desirable for exchange.

While the idea of paper currency was first brought up in the 7th century under the Shang Dynasty, paper currency in its physical form wasn't produced until the 11th century under the Song Dynasty. Prior to the use of paper currency, China utilized metal coins as their main currency. The coins were circular in shape and had a rectangular hole in the middle. This design enabled the coins to be kept together on a rope. For the rich in China, this rope with cones eventually gets to heavy to carry. The resolution for this problem was to leave your coins with another person and have a piece of paper stating how much money you left with the person. In the future, you could present this paper to the person holding your coins and get your money back. This concept laid the groundwork for the Song Dynasty's banknote called the jiaozi.

In the year 960, the Song Dynasty was running low on copper that were used for creating coins, so they issued the first banknotes. These notes represented a guarantee that the value will be redeemed at a later date. While jiaozi was used as a convenience, there existence didn't entirely phase out metal coins. The use of paper notes coincided with the use of coins.

Over time, the government of the Song Dynasty started seeing the benefits of implementing paper currencies into their economy. As a result, they dramatically increased the amount of notes being issued. During the 12th century, China's central government produced enough paper notes to equal 26 million coins strings. In the 1120's, the Chinese government started producing state owned paper currency.

Paper money first came to the United States in the late 1600's. The Massachusetts Bay Colony introduced the first paper currency to the United States on February 3, 1690. This money was issued to pay off war debts. Paper currency in the 1690's was classified as a bill of credit. This money enabled soldiers to trade it like gold and silver coins. In the year 1775, the leaders of several colonies tried to replicate the success of Massachusetts by producing large amounts of paper currency. The only problem was all of this paper money wasn't backed by any gold or silver coins. As a result, inflation quickly devalued the worth of this paper money.In the 1860's, the Civil War was supported by two different currencies. The Confederate used one currency and the Union used another. The values of these currencies went up and down throughout the duration of the war. After the Civil War, the United States government implemented a uniform monetary system where banks produced paper notes backed by government bonds. Over the next few decades, the other currencies where phased out in favor of paper currencies issued by national banks.

The advantages of paper currency over metal coins include it's lightweight, cost effective, and more portability. First, paper weighs less than metal, so it is easier to carry large amounts of it without it being to heavy. Second, paper currency is more cost effective than coins because it cost less to produce paper. Coins like nickels and pennies actually cost more to produce than they are worth, which makes it an inefficient investment. That is why countries like Canada have stopped producing pennies. Third, paper money is more portable because it is lightweight and can be placed in your wallet. This makes it more easy to transport and harder to lose.

The disadvantages of paper currency compared to coins is the fact that there are more durable, harder to counterfeit, and has intrinsic value. Paper money is susceptible to tears,rips, and fading. On the other hand, coins are tough to break and last forever. Paper currency's shelf life is no more than a few years, while coins can last for several centuries. Furthermore, the fact that it costs more to make coins than paper money deters criminals from counterfeiting it as frequently. Another benefit of coins over paper money is that it's easier for blind people to identify the difference between different values. For example, a blind person can not differentiate between a 20 dollar bill and a 100 dollar bill. But when it comes to coins, different coin values come in unique sizes and engravings. Due to the uniqueness of different coin denominations, the blind can easier identify the difference between coins. Moreover, coins were designed they way they are to assist individuals that are visually impaired.

In conclusion, many people were skeptical about paper currency when it was first introduced by the Chinese government. Many perceived paper currency as a bad thing because it didn't have any intrinsic value and wasn't durable. But fast forward several centuries, and it is the most popular form of currency in this world. This large turn around had to do with the fact the paper money is easier to handle, transport, and is cheaper to make. While using gold and silver coins as a primary currency stayed a tradition for several centuries, the world eventually evolved and got on board with a more cost effective monetary system.

Perhaps cryptocurrencies will one day be looked upon the same way.

CHAPTER THREE INVESTING IN CRYPTOCURRENCY

-Bitcoin is really a fascinating example of how human beings create value, and is not always rational... tt is not a rational currency in that case. -Alan Greenspan

INTRODUCTION

Cryptocurrencies are steadily becoming more and more accepted by all the key players in the financial sector. However, they are still in their infancy for a large part. For this reason, many would-be investors may not know how to get started in the acquisition and trade of these currencies.

This is the question we are going to answer in the proceeding discussions. We are going to let you know how to get started in the trade of the currency. We are going to do this by answering the following pertinent questions:

How do you go about investing in cryptocurrency? Can you do it all yourself or do you need a broker? How do you decide on the best currency to invest in? And should you go all in or is this a fad that will end?

HOW TO INVEST IN CRYPTOCURRENCY

Step I: Familiarize yourself with the ABCs of Cryptocurrency

Every discipline has its unique technical jargons and fundamental principles. The field of cryptocurrency is by no means an exception to this universal rule. Among the top terminologies, you ought to familiarize yourself with are blockchain, spread, cryptocurrency, wallet, and transaction fees.

This is because they are widely used in this trade. Familiarizing yourself with these terms will thus enhance your performance and overall experience in the process of trading.

Step II: Create a Cryptocurrency Wallet

Cryptocurrency wallets work more or less like the typical ordinary wallet. They enable you to receive, preserve, and send digital currency much like your ordinary wallet would do to your ordinary notes and coins.

Some of the top cryptocurrency wallets you might want to start with are KeepKey, Nano Ledger S, Trezor, Coinbase, MyEtherWallet, Jaxx, and Electrum. To create a wallet in any of these sites, you simply need to log in and input your full details, much like creating an ordinary online account.

Step III: Link your Bank Account to your Cryptocurrency Wallet

To deal in these cryptocurrencies, you will have to link your pre existing bank account to the wallet you have created. This is because, by their design and nature, the currencies can only be transacted via an online/electronic platform.

To link both accounts, your bank has to accept and support cryptocurrencies. You will then proceed to match your bank account number, your bank's routing number, and your full name as it appears on your bank account.

Step IV: Identify and Create an Account on the Right Exchange Platform

Exchange platforms are sites that pair up sellers of cryptocurrencies and their prospective buyers. They function much the same way as ordinary forex brokerage; the only difference being that they deal in cryptocurrencies rather than ordinary cash.

Among the highly reputable exchange platforms in vogue, today are Coinbase, Binance, Bittrex, Kraken, Cex.io, Coinmama, Bitstamp,

Poloniex, Coinone, and Gemini. Give them a topmost priority in your search for the right exchange platform.

Step V: Commence Trading

You are now set to go. You can now commence trading these cryptocurrencies. As a general rule, buy the cryptocurrencies when they have lower values and sell them when their values peak. This way, you shall derive some spread or profit.

Alternatively, you might also consider selling them when their prices are high and repurchasing them when their prices dip. To time your trading appropriately, you have to keep a keen eye on the latest market trends.

CAN YOU DO IT ALL YOURSELF OR DO YOU NEED A BROKER?

Inasmuch as investing in cryptocurrencies is largely a do-it-yourself activity, you might at times consider invoking the assistance of a broker. These are firms of individuals who are well-versed in the field of cryptocurrencies and who may subsequently assist you in going about the issue. The following are some of the benefits of seeking the assistance of a third party:

Faster

The entire process of setting up an account and trading will be faster than would ordinarily be the case. This is because the brokers have more experience and are also wholly dedicated to the setting up and running of these accounts. You will hence expend too little time and receive the benefits faster than usual.

Less Room for Error

Given that these brokers are more experienced in the field of cryptocurrencies, they are less likely to make any errors in the course of setting up the accounts. This is in sharp contrast to a situation in which you may have to do so yourself. For this reason, you are better off with a broker than going it alone. This is especially important if you are not well knowledgeable in the field of cryptocurrencies.

Adequate Support

These brokers also offer adequate backend support to you. These include such issues as further explanations, additional support, advisory, and consultancy services, among others. These extra supports will enrich your overall experience and ultimately greater profitability. By going it alone, you forfeit these benefits.

Effective Follow-up

After creating the account for you, you still might not have the wherewithal necessary to operate that account well. These brokers go beyond merely helping you get started. They are always on standby and quite eager to offer you the necessary support you need to make those baby steps perfectly well.On the flipside, these brokers have certain downsides. Below are two of the most outstanding of those:

Expensive

These brokers avail their services for a fee. It, therefore, follows that you will spend a lot of money while getting started in the trade should you opt to have them assist you. In the process, you will end up spending more than you would ordinarily have had you opted to go it alone.

Unnecessary Bureaucracy

Working with these brokers also entails some lengthy and sometimes unnecessary bureaucracy. This results in uncalled for delays that may subsequently pose unnecessary inconveniences. You are therefore advised to disregard the brokers in case you want to operate the accounts as a matter of urgency.

Conclusion

From the foregoing, it is better to work with brokers in case you are a complete novice in the field of cryptocurrencies. If you are an expert in the field, you are strongly advised to bypass them altogether. This shall save you a bit of time and money.

HOW DO YOU DECIDE ON THE BEST CURRENCY TO INVEST IN?

With so many cryptocurrencies in circulation today, a would-be investor like you may often be at odds as to which exactly suits his unique preferences. Below are some of those factors you might want to pay attention to while selecting the most suitable one:

Exchangeability

This refers to the likelihood that the said cryptocurrency can be converted into ordinary currency. Most exchange platforms deal with only a handful of cryptocurrencies such as Etherum and Bitcoin. Also, many jurisdictions and financial markets world over are yet to fully embrace this concept of cryptocurrencies altogether. You should thus ascertain that the cryptocurrency of choice is supported by your country's financial systems.

Liquidity

Liquidity is the sum total of those cryptocurrencies in the market. Higher liquidity means ease and convenience of trading and vice versa. To ascertain a cryptocurrency's liquidity, you will have to look out for other users in your country, locality, or financial ecosystem. Choose a currency that has a higher acceptance rate to be able to enjoy this benefit.

Safety and Security

Cryptocurrencies are more prone to the breach of security than probably all the other forms of exchanges. They are particularly susceptible to identity theft and internet downturns. You should, therefore, see to it that the currency you decide to settle on has a full backing. It should further be highly encrypted, authenticated, and demand verification before any transaction can be effected.

Customer Support

From time to time, issues may often arise while transacting businesses via these cryptocurrencies. These include sending the amount to the wrong account, unauthorized access of your money, and identity theft, among others. A good cryptocurrency has to be backed by 24/7 backend customer support that shields you from the aforementioned side effects.

Transaction Fees

All these issuers of these cryptocurrencies do levy some fees to facilitate transactions and offer the needed support. However, the amount of fees levied varies largely from one currency to another. This has an impact on the profit or disposable income you might possibly derive out of their usage or adoption. Look out for that cryptocurrency that has the lowest possible transaction fee.

SHOULD YOU GO ALL IN OR IS THIS A FAD THAT WILL END?

The whole concept of cryptocurrency is largely in its infancy. The first cryptocurrency was issued just the other day (June 2009). This means that we are yet to see what the whole concept or technology may have in store for humanity.

Going forward, the field of cryptocurrency is likely to witness more players, more trading opportunities, and a higher number of users worldwide. This shall lead to lower profit margins but greater safety and overall acceptability.

Cryptocurrencies are undoubtedly the currencies of the future. They are going to be the standard commonly accepted means of exchange in future. In light of this, you are by all means strongly advised to adopt them soonest possible.

CONCLUSION

It is our hope that the information we have furnished above is insightful and informative to you. Cryptocurrencies are indeed the way to go for any shrewd investor who wishes to leverage greater profit margins and stay in business long enough.

CHAPTER FOUR THE RISK OF INVESTING IN CRYPTOCURRENCIES

BITCOIN AND CRYPTOCURRENCY

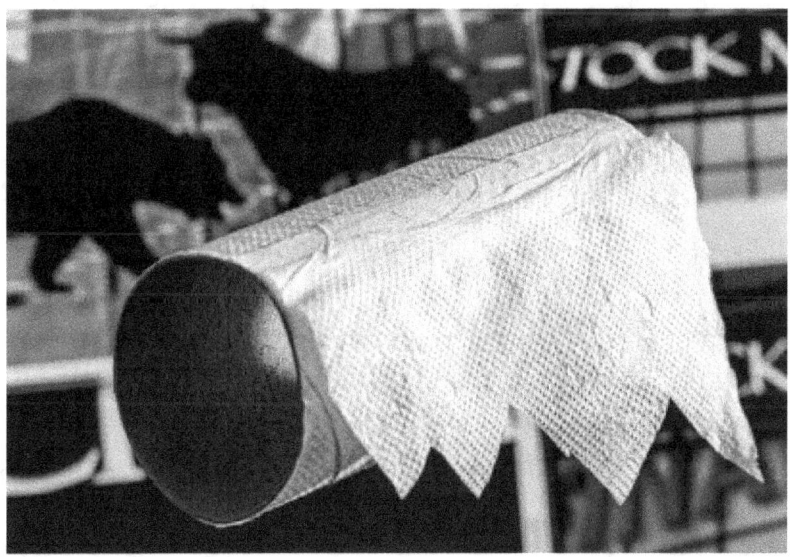

-I do not understand where the backing of Bitcoin is coming from. There is no fundamental issue of capabilities of repaying it in anything which is universally acceptable, which is either intrinsic value of the currency or the credit or trust of the individual who is issuing the money, whether it's a government or an individual. -Alan Greenspan

When it comes to investing in Cryptocurrencies, many people think of it as the best way of making quick money. The truth is that recently, people made lots of money from the bitcoin currency, which means it may be true that investing in Cryptocurrencies may be the best way of making money. What you should keep in mind is that these are complex concepts that require you to take some time to understand them.

Some new forms of digital currency are being launched, meaning you need to be careful. One huge mistake is deciding to invest in Cryptocurrencies before you figure out how they work. No matter the type of currency you choose to invest in, for example, bitcoin, you need to have an in-depth understanding of how investing is done.

Cryptocurrencies aren't controlled or regulated by the government, meaning many individuals think they are illegal. They are not physical money, but digital currency. It means you can't exchange it at the ATM. On the other hand, these currencies are not illegal. It's important you know these factors before you decide to invest in cryptocurrency. In this informative post, we'll look at the risks of investing in these forms of digital currencies.

1. You Can Lose Money

One thing you should remember is that Cryptocurrencies are a young market, meaning their prices fluctuate at alarming rates. If you haven't gathered enough facts to invest in them, for example, bitcoin, you may end up losing your money, that's before the market corrects itself. Professional investors in Cryptocurrencies may also not be aware or be able to predict a market crash, which means all you have to do is hope for the best. It is one practice you don't want to depend on if it's your money at stake.

2. You Can Get Hacked

The cryptocurrency market is a digital world, meaning you're never sure of getting the best returns. For instance, skilled and smart hackers can hack your account and take all your money. You should ensure you take precautions on the platforms you're on. Keep in mind one of the most significant risks when it comes to cryptocurrency investing is hacking; which means you should be careful.

3. You Can't Know the Source Of The Money

Cryptocurrencies are not regulated by governments, which means you can get money from internet terrorists without knowing, for example, if you are a frequent user of the dark web. If the government or other authorities track the money and find it in your account, you can find yourself in some rough place. If you are an inexperienced first-time investor, you may be unable to explain the source of the money. It could mean you remain on the authorities' radar for some time, which is not a good scenario for investors.

4. You Can Be Conned

If you use your credit card to buy items and realize later you have been scammed, you can choose to call your bank and get back the surplus you paid for. In the best instances, the bank will refund you the money. However, if you lose money when trading in cryptocurrency, for example with bitcoin transactions, you won't be able to get any help. Erroneous or illegal trades are hard to trace over the internet, which you need to be aware of.

5. You Can Be Scammed

The cryptocurrency market is highly volatile, meaning you have no guarantee you will get particular gains. It's among the most unrealistic trades, which means if you are an inexperienced investor, you may find yourself being ripped off. By investing in Cryptocurrencies, you have no guarantee you will get any profits, which means you may be getting into what is referred to as a "Ponzi scheme". The best way to invest in the bitcoin currency is to gather as much information as you can before spending money. It will prevent you from getting into trouble and losing your money.

Conclusion

Investing in Cryptocurrencies requires you to research extensively before spending your money. Just as with any other trade or business plan, you need to ensure you do careful planning and have a will to take risks. For instance, when investing in the bitcoin currency, you should bear in mind that if you lose your money, you will have no chance of getting back your money.

Among the downsides of investing in Cryptocurrencies is that they have high volatility and low liquidity, which means you shouldn't spend money if you have no idea on how the process works. For the best outcome, you should watch some seminars or tutorials. Another tip is to look for people who have been investing for a long time and have them explain to you how the process works.

CHAPTER FIVE BITCOIN GOLD 2.0?

Bitcoin is a snippet of code representing ownership of a digital concept. Its main feature is that it doesn't have a central regulating body where payments pass through. It's also not controlled by any government and thus can be used for transactions across borders. For a commodity to be used as currency, there are some major characteristics that it must have and these are: stability, reliability, general acceptability, durability, long history of acceptance and are inherently valuable. These are the characteristics that we are going to compare the Bitcoin and gold against to see if indeed Bitcoin has the capability of substituting gold as the go-to currency in terms of crisis.

In terms of stability, gold has been around for more than 3000 years and has been used as the store of wealth with its value remaining ever high over that period. On the other hand, the value of Bitcoins in the market has kept fluctuating and this does not inspire confidence for a commodity that's supposedly on its way to becoming the world's future currency. In the past few months, the value of Bitcoins has gone up by up to 49% before succumbing to recent turbulence. The change in its value has been mostly upwards but such inconsistencies make the Bitcoin's stability low offering investors little guarantee of the security of their investments. The changes in the exchange rates between major currencies are usually low and rarely over 5% within a month which is clearly not the case with the Bitcoins.

When we check on reliability, Bitcoins rely on the internet and any crackdown by a foreign government can hugely affect the business and lead to losses. This is not the case with gold which is not dependent on the internet and is not affected by the technological disruptions. It has withstood the test of time over the years and it's highly probable that 100 years down the line, its supply will still be there and it will still be valuable.

For any transaction to take place we must have a willing buyer and seller and this means that the Bitcoin still has a long way to go since many people and organizations still don't use Bitcoins as currency. This is mainly because they are new and lack a long history of acceptance. Many countries are still getting used to the idea and very few big institutions comfortably use Bitcoins for their transactions in business dealings. Other countries like France have an issue with the digital currency because of the lack of identity of the parties conducting the transactions which is against their laws.

This also brings to the fore the issue of legality of the Bitcoin system. We have countries like Japan which view Bitcoin positively but most of the countries are wary of the dangers poised through the system and have put in place measures to ensure safe transactions. Other countries like Israel are seeking introduction of tax on Bitcoin. Bitcoin is also legal in countries like the US, Canada, Australia while others like the UK and Switzerland plan to advance regulatory framework favoring cryptocurrency. The lack of general acceptability, at least for now, means that the chances of Bitcoin being adopted as world's currency become even less.

Transactions made on Bitcoin are slow and therefore inconvenient as a means of currency. This is because there is a limit on the number of transactions to be conducted per day and the identity of the transacting parties has to be concealed which ultimately means that a simple transaction may take days to complete. This is another barrier that stands in the way of Bitcoin.

Another distinct difference between the cryptocurrencies and gold is that unlike the cryptocurrencies, gold has its own value while Bitcoin is only as much as people are willing to pay. This makes Bitcoins more suited for short term investment where people buy expecting its value to rise in the future. Bitcoins are therefore not viewed so much as long term investments as is the case with gold and other precious metals and therefore cannot serve in the long term due to the high risk involved as compared to the significantly lower risk of gold and other precious metals.

Despite Bitcoins higher utility in this technological era, gold still retains the upper hand over the long haul and this is mainly due to the high risk that comes with the Bitcoins. A lack of stability and reliability coupled with the lack of widespread acceptability doom the Bitcoin in this competition. Bitcoin still has some ground to cover in convincing people that it can be trusted yet past history involving other big busts like the Dutch tulips, NASDAQ and Japanese real estate suggests that we will only have one winner in the long term, Gold.

CHAPTER SIX OTHER CRYPTOCURRENCIES

-Make no mistake - Ethereum would never have existed without Bitcoin as a forerunner. That said, I think Ethereum is ahead of Bitcoin in many ways and represents the bleeding edge of digital currency. - Fred Ehrsam

Bitcoin hit the media with a vengeance. All of the sudden, people were talking about how this unregulated (well, semi-regulated) currency has appreciated in value by %1000. For example, if a person bought bitcoin at $100, the coin was worth $10 000 a few years later. However, the height and hype of bitcoin has worn down. Now, there are other cryptocurrencies that are making waves. The following is a list of a few of the major players and a list of pro's and con's for each:

Ethereum

Ethereum is a platform for users to build decentralized software in the form of apps. Miners will work for Ether.

Pro's

-Great for those interested in new forms of knowledge creation
-Accessible to those who understand computer technology
-A viable alternative for those frustrated with the Internet
-A reactionary product to net neutrality

Con's

-There is no currency like Bitcoin (Ether is not directly translatable into cash)

-A complex interface that lacks the sophistication and user friendliness of the web

-There is no regulation as of yet regarding the type of content available to users

Litecoin

Litecoin was established in 2011. It is a peer to peer system. Like Bitcoin, it is digital gold in a sense. It allows businesses and people to transfer funds to each other without going through any banks.

Pro's

-Is 3/4's faster than Bitcoin

-Transactions are confirmed very quickly

-One of the top 5 crypto currencies

-Can be purchased through the website Coinbase

Con's

-Mining is more expensive than Bitcoin

-Complicated to create

-Less rare than Bitcoin even though production of the coins has stopped

Monero

Monero is a type of crypto currency that uses specific cryptography to ensure that its paths are untraceable. It all began in July 2012. It is headed by seven developers, five of which are anonymous. The other two are named David Latapie and Riccardo Spagni. This currency is funded through crowds.

Pro's

-Completely untraceable money pathways and transactions

-Your identity remains private when you spend your money

-All the money is clean

Con's

-Is prime fascia real estate for money launderers

-There is no way to prove really that a person has paid for anything
-It is not an easy currency for beginners to adopt

Zcash

Zcash is a lot like Bitcoin but it is completely anonymous. No one is able to trace paths of those who buy and sell. It is new as it launched on the 28th of October 2016. It has a whole team of people working on it including Roger Ver, Barry Seibert, and Pantera Capital. However the entire operation is set up like a company and not as a community like the other currencies.

Pro's
-Has the potential to be huge like Bitcoin
-The money has first been backed by investors

Con's
-Can feed into neoliberalism
-You have to give some of your profits back to the company (20%)
-Has been accused of simply lining the pockets of corporations

When choosing cryptocurrencies, the list is endless. There are currencies that are now being developed every day. TC has a comprehensive list of the existing ones, and they are too many to just list off (https://techcrunch.com/2017/11/19/100-cryptocurrencies-described-in-4-words-or-less/). The site also gives a four word description of what each currency is. However, it can be difficult to rely on just four words to describe such a complex subject.

However, the point is that people might have felt left out of Bitcoin. It is very mainstream now and everyone knows that it is worth a lot of money. Most people who didn't get in at the beginning are kicking themselves. But they should also be encouraged that this is just the beginning in a long list of developments. Trading goods and services has become increasingly complex. If people would have said ten years ago to someone that there would be new forms of money developed, many would have just scoffed. It is difficult to conceive of the concept in a world that was not as digital. People were still worried about the safety and reliability of the Internet. Now they flock there to buy new forms of currency untraceable by the government. The above list represents just some of the opportunities that are affordable right now in the glow of Bitcoin's great success.

-Ethereum exists because it enables developers to write smart contracts better than Bitcoin in the near-term. Zcash will exist because it will attempt to do privacy better than Bitcoin in the near-term, and the token gives you access to the anonymity protocol. - Nick Tomaino

CHAPTER SEVEN BLOCKCHAIN TECHNOLOGY

BITCOIN AND CRYPTOCURRENCY

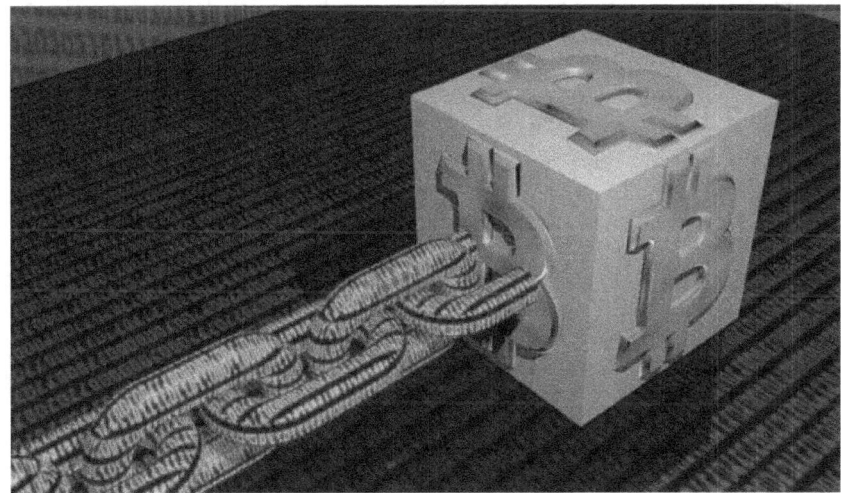

When you drill down, blockchains are really a shared version of reality everyone agrees on. So whether it's a fully immersive VR experience, augmented reality, or even Bitcoin or Ethereum in the physical world as a shared ledger for our 'real world,' we'll increasingly trust blockchains as our basis for reality. Fred Ehrsam

Is blockchain technology the new web?

The blockchain is a certainly quick development – the brainchild of individuals known as, Nakamoto. Be that as it may, from that point forward, it has advanced into something more noteworthy, and the fundamental inquiry each and every individual is asking is: What is Blockchain?

By enabling advanced data to be conveyed however not duplicated, blockchain technology made the foundation of another sort of web. Initially contrived for the computerized cash, Bitcoin, (Buy Bitcoin) the tech group is presently finding other potential uses for the technology.

Bitcoin has been called "computerized gold," and for a justifiable reason. To date, the aggregate estimation of the money is near $9 billion US. What's more, blockchains can influence different sorts of computerized to esteem. Like the web (or your auto), you don't have to know how the blockchain attempts to utilize it. Be that as it may, having a fundamental information of this new technology indicates why it's viewed as progressive. In this way, we trust you appreciate this, what is Blockchain manage.

What is Blockchain Technology?

The blockchain is a morally sound computerized record of monetary exchanges that can be customized to record not simply budgetary exchanges but rather basically everything of esteem.

An appropriated database

Picture a spreadsheet that is copied a huge number of times over a system of PCs. At that point envision that this system is intended to consistently refresh this spreadsheet and you have an essential comprehension of the blockchain

information hung on a blockchain exists as a common — and persistently accommodated — database. This is a method for utilizing the system that has evident advantages. The blockchain database isn't put away in any single area, which means the records it keeps are genuinely open and effortlessly obvious. No incorporated variant of this data exists for a programmer to degenerate. Facilitated by a great many PCs all the while, its information is available to anybody on the web.

To run in more profound with the similarity to Google spreadsheet, I may require you to look over this piece from a blockchain master.

Blockchain as Google Docs

The customary method for offering records to joint effort is to send a Microsoft Word archive to another beneficiary, and request that they make modifications to it. The issue with that situation is that you have to hold up until the point when getting an arrival duplicate before you can see or roll out different improvements since you are bolted out of altering it until the point when the other individual is finished with it. That is the way databases work today. Two proprietors can't be upsetting a similar record at once. That's the manner by which banks keep up cash adjusts and exchanges; they quickly bolt access (or abatement the adjust) while they make an exchange, at that point refresh the opposite side, at that point re-open access (or refresh again). With Google Docs (or Google

Sheets), the two gatherings approach a similar archive in the meantime, and the single variant of that report is constantly obvious to them two. It resembles a common record, however it is a mutual report. The appropriated part becomes possibly the most important factor when sharing includes various individuals.

Envision the quantity of authoritative records that ought to be utilized that way. Rather than passing them to each other, forgetting about renditions, and not being in a state of harmony with the other adaptation, for what reason can't *all* business archives end up shared rather than exchanged forward and backward? Such huge numbers of sorts of legitimate contracts would be perfect for that sort of workflow.You need not bother with a blockchain to share archives, yet the common reports relationship is an intense one

Blockchain Durability and heartiness

Blockchain technology resembles the web in that it has a worked in power. By putting away pieces of data that are indistinguishable over its system, the blockchain can't:

1. Be controlled by any single substance.
2. Has no single purpose of disappointment.

Bitcoin was designed in 2008. Since that time, the Bitcoin blockchain has worked without noteworthy disturbance. (To date, any of issues related with Bitcoin have been because of hacking or blunder. As such, these issues originate from terrible goal and human mistake, not blemishes in the basic ideas.)

The web itself has ended up being strong for very nearly 30 years. It's a reputation that looks good for blockchain technology as it keeps on being created.

Straightforward and ethical

The blockchain organize lives in a condition of accord, one that naturally checks in with itself at regular intervals. A sort of self-evaluating environment of an advanced esteem, the system accommodates each exchange that occurs in ten-minute interims. Each gathering of these exchanges is alluded to as a "piece". Two essential properties result from this:

1. Transparency information is inserted inside the system all in all, by definition it is open.

2. It can't be undermined modifying any unit of data on the blockchain would mean utilizing a colossal measure of processing energy to supersede the whole system.

In principle, this could be conceivable. By and by, it's probably not going to happen. Taking control of the framework to catch Bitcoins, for example, would likewise have the impact of devastating their value.

blockchain takes care of the issue of control. When I talk about it in the West, individuals say they put stock in Google, Facebook, or their banks. Yet, whatever is left of the world doesn't trust associations and enterprises that much — I mean Africa, India, the Eastern Europe, or Russia. It's not about the spots where individuals are extremely rich. Blockchain's chances are the most astounding in the nations that haven't achieved that level yet.

A system of hubs

A system of alleged figuring "hubs" make up the blockchain.

Hub : (PC associated with the blockchain organize utilizing a customer that plays out the undertaking of approving and transferring exchanges) gets a duplicate of the blockchain, which gets downloaded consequently after joining the blockchain arrange.

Together they make an effective second-level system, a completely extraordinary vision for how the web can work.

Each hub is a "chairman" of the blockchain, and joins the system deliberately (in this sense, the system is decentralized). Be that as it may, everyone has a motivator for partaking in the system: the possibility of winning Bitcoins.

Hubs are said to be "mining" Bitcoin, however the term is something of a misnomer. Indeed, every one is contending to win Bitcoins by explaining computational riddles. Bitcoin was the raison d'etre of the blockchain as it was initially imagined. It's presently perceived to be just the first of numerous potential uses of the technology.

There are an expected 700 Bitcoin-like digital forms of money (interchangeable esteem tokens) officially accessible. Also, a scope of other potential adjustments of the first blockchain idea are presently dynamic, or being developed.

The possibility of decentralization

By outline, the blockchain is a decentralized technology.

Anything that occurs on it is a component of the system all in all. Some imperative ramifications originate from this. By making another approach to confirm exchanges parts of conventional business could wind up superfluous. Securities exchange exchanges turn out to be relatively concurrent on the blockchain, for example — or it could make sorts of record keeping, similar to a land registry, completely open. What's more, decentralization is as of now a reality.

A worldwide system of PCs utilizes blockchain technology to together deal with the database that records Bitcoin exchanges. That is, Bitcoin is overseen by its system, and no one focal specialist. Decentralization implies the system works on a client to-client (or shared) premise. The types of mass joint effort this makes conceivable are simply starting to be explored.

Who will utilize the blockchain?

As web framework, you don't have to think about the blockchain for it to be valuable in your life.

At present, fund offers the most grounded utilize cases for the technology. Universal settlements, for example. The World Bank assesses that over $430 billion US in cash moves were sent in 2015. Also, right now there is a popularity for blockchain designers.

The blockchain conceivably removes the broker for these sorts of exchanges. Individualized computing ended up open to the overall population with the development of the Graphical User Interface (GUI), which appeared as a "work area". So also, the most well-known GUI formulated for the blockchain are the alleged "wallet" applications, which individuals use to purchase things with Bitcoin, and store it alongside different digital currencies.

Exchanges online are firmly associated with the procedures of personality confirmation. It is anything but difficult to envision that wallet applications will change in the coming a long time to incorporate different sorts of personality administration.

The Blockchain and Enhanced security

By putting away information over its system, the blockchain wipes out the dangers that accompany information being held halfway.

Its system needs concentrated purposes of defenselessness that PC programmers can misuse. The present web has security issues that are commonplace to everybody. We as a whole depend on the "username/secret word" framework to ensure our character and resources on the web. Blockchain security strategies utilize encryption technology.

The reason for this are the alleged open and private "keys". An "open key" (a long, arbitrarily produced series of numbers) is a client's' address on the blockchain. Bitcoins sent over the system gets recorded as having a place with that address. The "private key" resembles a secret key that gives its proprietor access to their Bitcoin or other advanced resources. Store your information on the blockchain and it is morally sound. This is valid, albeit securing your computerized resources will likewise require defending of your private key by printing it out, making what's alluded to as a paper wallet.

The Blockchain a New Web 3.0?

The blockchain enables web clients to make esteem and verifies advanced data. What will new business applications result?

Savvy contracts

Dispersed records empower the coding of straightforward contracts that will execute when indicated conditions are met. Ethereum is an open source blockchain venture that was manufactured particularly to understand this plausibility. All things considered, in its beginning periods, Ethereum can possibly use the value of blockchains on a really world-evolving scale.

At the technology's present level of improvement, shrewd contracts can be customized to perform straightforward capacities. For example, a subsidiary could be paid out when a money related instrument meets certain benchmark, with the utilization of blockchain technology and Bitcoin empowering the payout to be robotized.

The sharing economy

With organizations like Uber and AirBnB prospering, the sharing economy is now a demonstrated achievement. At present, be that as it may, clients who need to hail a ride-sharing administration need to depend on a middle person like Uber. By empowering distributed installments, the blockchain opens the way to coordinate collaboration between parties — a really decentralized sharing economy comes about.

An early illustration, OpenBazaar utilizes blockchain technology to make a shared eBay. Download the application onto your smart phone or other device, and you will be able to conduct business with OpenBazaar sellers without paying exchange expenses. The "no principles" ethos of the convention implies that individual notoriety will be considerably more essential to business collaborations than it presently is on eBay.

Crowdfunding

Crowdfunding activities like Kickstarter and Gofundme are doing the propel work for the developing shared economy. The notoriety of these destinations recommends individuals need to have an immediate say in item advancement. Blockchains take this enthusiasm to the following level, possibly making swarm sourced investment reserves.

In 2016, one such examination, the Ethereum-based DAO (Decentralized Autonomous Organization), raised a bewildering $200 million USD in a little more than two months. Members obtained "DAO tokens" enabling them to vote on savvy contract funding ventures (voting power was proportionate to the quantity of DAO they were holding). A resulting hack of venture reserves demonstrated that the undertaking was propelled without appropriate due constancy, with appalling outcomes. In any case, the DAO test proposes the blockchain can possibly introduce "another worldview of financial collaboration."

Administration

By making the outcomes completely straightforward and openly available, conveyed database technology could convey full straightforwardness to races or some other sort of survey taking. Ethereum-based brilliant contracts help to mechanize and to monetize the procedure.

The application, Boardroom, empowers authoritative basic leadership to occur on the blockchain. By and by, this implies organization administration turns out to be completely straightforward and unquestionable while overseeing advanced resources, value or data.

Production network examining

Buyers progressively need to realize that the moral cases organizations make about their items are genuine. Disseminated records give a simple method to guarantee that the backstories of the things we purchase are authentic. Straightforwardness accompanies blockchain-based timestamping of a date and area — on moral jewels, for example — that compares to an item number.

The UK-based Provenance offers inventory network reviewing for a scope of customer merchandise. Making utilization of the Ethereum blockchain, a Provenance pilot venture guarantees that fish sold in Sushi eateries in Japan has been reasonably collected by its providers in Indonesia.

Record stockpiling

Decentralizing record stockpiling on the web brings clear advantages. Conveying information all through the system shields documents from getting hacked or lost.

Bury Planetary File System (IPFS) makes it simple to conceptualize how a conveyed web may work. Like the way a bittorrent moves information around the web, IPFS disposes of the requirement for unified customer server connections (i.e., the present web). A web made up of totally decentralized sites can possibly accelerate document exchange and gushing circumstances. Such a change isn't just helpful. It's a fundamental move up to the web's at present over-burden content-conveyance frameworks.

Expectation markets

The crowdsourcing of expectations on occasion likelihood is demonstrated to have a high level of exactness. Averaging assessments offsets the unexamined predispositions that misshape judgment. Expectation advertises that payout as per occasion results are as of now dynamic. Blockchains are a "shrewdness of the group" technology that will no uncertainty find different applications in the years to come.

In any case, in Beta, the forecast showcase application Augur makes share offerings on the result of genuine occasions. Members can gain cash by becoming tied up with the right expectation. The more offers acquired in the right result, the higher the payout will be. With a little responsibility of assets (not as much as a dollar), anybody can make an inquiry, make a market in light of an anticipated result, and gather half of all exchange expenses the market creates.

Assurance of licensed innovation

As is outstanding, advanced data can be interminably duplicated — and disseminated broadly because of the web. This has given web clients comprehensively a goldmine of free substance. Notwithstanding, copyright holders have not been so fortunate, losing control over their protected innovation and enduring fiscally as an outcome. Keen contracts can ensure copyright and robotize the offer of innovative works internet, dispensing with the danger of record duplicating and redistribution.

Mycelia utilizes the blockchain to make a shared music circulation framework. Established by the UK vocalist lyricist Imogen Heap, Mycelia empowers artists to offer melodies specifically to gatherings of people, and also permit tests to makers and divvy up eminences to lyricists and performers — these capacities being robotized by brilliant contracts. The limit of blockchains to issue installments in fragmentary digital money sums (micropayments) recommends this utilization case for the blockchain has a solid shot of achievement.

Web of Things (IoT)

What is the IoT? The system controlled administration of specific kinds of electronic gadgets — for example, the observing of air temperature in a storeroom. Savvy contracts make the robotization of remote frameworks administration conceivable. A mix of programming, sensors, and the system encourages a trade of information amongst articles and components. The outcome expands framework proficiency and enhances cost checking.

The greatest players in assembling, tech and broadcast communications are altogether competing for IoT strength. Think Samsung, IBM and AT&T. A characteristic augmentation of existing framework controlled by officeholders, IoT applications will run the range from prescient support of mechanical parts to information investigation, and mass-scale robotized frameworks administration.

Neighborhood Microgrids

Blockchain technology empowers the purchasing and offering of the sustainable power source created by neighborhood microgrids. At the point when sun oriented boards make abundance vitality, Ethereum-based brilliant contracts consequently redistribute it. Comparative sorts of shrewd contract mechanization will have numerous different applications as the IoT turns into a reality.

Situated in Brooklyn, Consensys is one of the preeminent organizations all inclusive that is building up a scope of utilizations for Ethereum. One anticipate they are joining forces on is Transactive Grid, working with the circulated vitality equip, LO3. A model task as of now up and running uses Ethereum brilliant contracts to mechanize the observing and redistribution of microgrid vitality. This supposed "shrewd matrix" is an early case of IoT usefulness.

Personality administration

There is a distinct requirement for better personality administration on the web. The capacity to confirm your character is the lynchpin of money related exchanges that happen on the web. In any case, solutions for the security chances that accompany web business are flawed, best case scenario. Circulated records offer upgraded strategies for demonstrating your identity, alongside the likelihood to digitize individual archives. Having a safe personality will likewise be vital for online associations — for example, in the sharing economy. A decent notoriety, all things considered, is the most critical condition for leading exchanges on the web.

Creating advanced character norms is turned out to be a profoundly complex process. Specialized difficulties aside, an all inclusive online personality arrangement requires participation between private substances and government. Add to that the need to explore lawful frameworks in various nations and the issue turns out to be exponentially troublesome. Web based business on the web right now depends on the SSL endorsement (the little green bolt) for secure exchanges on the web. Netki is a startup that tries to make a SSL standard for the blockchain. Having as of late declared a $3.5 million seed round, Netki expects an item dispatch in mid 2017.

AML and KYC

Against tax evasion (AML) and know your client (KYC) rehearses have a solid potential for being adjusted to the blockchain. As of now, budgetary foundations must play out a work concentrated multi-step process for each new client. KYC expenses could be lessened through cross-foundation customer check, and in the meantime increment observing and examination viability.

Startup Polycoin has an AML/KYC arrangement that includes breaking down exchanges. Those exchanges distinguished as being suspicious are sent on to consistence officers. Another startup Tradle is building up an application called Trust in Motion (TiM). Described as an "Instagram for KYC", TiM enables clients to take a preview of key archives (international ID, service charge, and so forth.). Once checked by the bank, this information is cryptographically put away on the blockchain.

Don't miss out!

Click the button below and you can sign up to receive emails whenever rodney cannon publishes a new book. There's no charge and no obligation.

https://books2read.com/r/B-A-YPE-YGZR

BOOKS 2 READ

Connecting independent readers to independent writers.

Did you love *BITCOIN AND CRYPTOCURRENCY*? Then you should read *On Writing A Low Budget Screenplay* by rodney cannon!

On Writing A Low Budget Screenplay will not only offer advice and rules that must be followed if you wish to craft a script that can be produced for a few thousand dollars, but how to look at your script from the view of the film maker. This book is short and to the point. It does not take more words to tell you how to write a low budget script than are actually in one.

Read more at cannondigitalfeaturefilmmaking.blogspot.com.

Also by rodney cannon

30 Days Cooking series
Cooking With Strawberries, 30 Days of Cool Recipes

BITTER WATERS SUITE
Bitter Waters Suite, Episode One
Bitter Waters Suite, Episode Two, Reasons to Believe

Blockchain Technologies
BITCOIN AND CRYPTOCURRENCY

Empires Falling Short Stories
Hunting The Hand
Empires Falling, The Land of the Khan
The First Port In The Storm
Whispers From A Speaking Demon

microwave cooking

Cooking With Mic, 25 Easy Microwave Recipes and More
Desserts With Mic

PARANORMAL INVESTIGATORS

Paranormal Investigators ed And Lorraine Warren, The Enfield Poltergeist
Paranormal Investigators 2, Amityville An Ed and Lorraine Warren File
Paranormal Investigators 3 The Exorcist, Father Gabriele Amoth
Paranormal Investigators The Collection Books 6 - 10

The serial killers
The Serial Killers, Pure Evil
The Serial Killers Collection

Standalone
On Writing A Low Budget Screenplay
Running An Online Business, Ending the Confusion
On Low Budget Film Making, Digital Film Making Interviews
Calling Vicki
The Micro Budget Film Making Collection
Cooking With Ketchup, 30 Go To Recipes

Watch for more at cannondigitalfeaturefilmmaking.blogspot.com.

www.ingramcontent.com/pod-product-compliance
Lightning Source LLC
Chambersburg PA
CBHW030053230526
45471CB00003B/1076